BECOME THE YOUNGEST BUSINESSPERSON IN TOWN

111 TEEN BUSINESS

IDEAS

*From Simple $100 Plans to
Great Personal Projects*

Thomas Henderson

has been derived from various sources. Please consult a licensed professional before attempting any techniques outlined in this book.

By reading this document, the reader agrees that under no circumstances is the author responsible for any losses, direct or indirect, which are incurred as a result of the use of the information contained herein; including, but not limited to, errors, omissions, or inaccuracies.

Table of Contents

Introduction

Being a teenager is the prime age to start your own business. You have the energy, the zeal, and the creativity to keep your business rolling. Yet due to the limitation of capital, many teens are dissuaded from starting their businesses.

However, the real limitation is not a lack of capital but a lack of information. Information is power, and much more powerful than capital. I don't mean that you should start a business without capital (even though you can), but I mean that you don't need loads of cash to do so. With $100, you can be ready to go.

There are many businesses that you can start with $100 or less. Succeeding in business is a combination of capital, labor, and creativity. You have plenty of labor and creativity— a lack of capital should not hold you back.

In this book, I am going to provide you with more than 100 business ideas that you can implement with $100 or less. Out of all these entrepreneurial options, you are sure to find one that you have the skills, passion, and the required creativity to convert into a stable business.

PART I: SERVICE PROVISION BUSINESSES

Do you have something that you can serve others with? Is there something that your family, friends, and loved ones like receiving from you?

Is there something that you are passionate about doing for others?

The easiest thing you can make money from is serving others with what you are passionate about.

Identify Your Service

I don't know what service you are good at offering. Sometimes, you yourself may not even realize that there are certain services that you can offer. To help you take stock of what you can offer, I have listed several of them in this book.

Quick criteria to guide you in the kind of services you can offer are:

➤ You have the skills, knowledge, and competence to perform it.

➤ You have the passion and confidence to perform it.

➤ There is a demand for this service.

➤ Your service is monetizable.

➤ You can afford to deliver it.

Monetizing Your Service

Everyone serves others. No one doesn't serve others or is incapable of serving others. This is part of the inherent nature in every human being. You are not an exception. However, most of us serve for free. Most of us do not know how to make money from serving others.

Change your mindset about money

Some of us are beholden to the negative belief that there are certain things that we cannot do for money. Thus, we end up broke, yet work hard to offer free services.

To monetize your service, stop these limiting beliefs. Change your mindset. See monetizing your service as a way of replenishing your service stock. For you to serve, you have to eat, you have to bathe, you have to wear clothes, you have to find a place to sleep. All of these are expenses. Whether it is you bearing them or your parents, it doesn't matter. They have to be paid for. So why should you incur the expenses and yet dispense free service? It makes no sense.

Start quantifying your service in saleable form

Once you have identified services that you can offer, the next thing is to quantify your service in a saleable form. Ask yourself, "How much am I going to offer for $1?"

The following are some of the ways to quantify your money:

➢ Based on time
➢ Based on piecework
➢ Based on a combination of time and piecework

Make Your Service Deliverable

Ask yourself, "Where do people need my service?" For some services, clients will come to you. And for some services, you will have to go to the clients. For others, you can make some mutual arrangement to meet halfway at some third-party place. What is important is that you can deliver your service to a place that boosts your client's satisfaction.

Get Clients

Once you have been able to make your service deliverable, the next logical step is to deliver the service to the clients. Depending on the kind of service, you will either go to the clients or the clients will have to come to you. For some services, it can work both ways.

Face-to-face services are limited in terms of geographic scope. On the other hand, services that do not need face-to-face encounters are not limited by geographic scope. For example, working as a virtual assistant has no geographic limit.

Get Paid

Before marketing your service, you must ensure that there are working channels through which you can receive funds. This is not a big deal if the services are localized and need face-to-face encounters. However, when it comes to services that are delivered across different countries, then payment channels become of utmost importance.

For international clients, you will need international bank transfers through the SWIFT system. Alternatively, you can use PayPal, Stripe, or other such payment methods available in both your country and your clients' country.

Transform Your Service Into a Business

This book is not about making you self-employed, but about making you a TEEN BUSINESS ENTREPRENEUR. Of course, being self-employed is the first step. But this shouldn't be the last step.

What differentiates being self-employed from being in business?

Being self-employed is about **working for money**. The reward you get is simply a **wage**.

Being in business is about **letting money work for you**. The reward you get is **profit**.

How do you let money work for you? When it comes to service, the first step is using money to get people with the right knowledge, information, and skills work on your behalf. You might as well be part of a working team, but it is not about "self" rather, it is about "business." Instead of being "self-employed" you are "business-employed."

Chapter 1: Providing Knowledge, Skills, and Information Services

We are in the age of knowledge. Our knowledge economy continues to grow exponentially. Why not claim a piece of this pie?

There will always be something that you know that others don't. Discover what that knowledge and information is. It could be a language. It could be about your special location. It could be about your unique culture. It could be about your personal experience. The list is limitless.

Let me give you a few hints just to trigger your mind to think of many others unlisted here.

Training, Tutoring, and Mentoring Businesses

Training, tutoring, and mentoring businesses are part of the multi-billion dollar education industry. Provided you have the knowledge or information and the skill to deliver it, you can never fail to be rewarded handsomely.

The following are some of the niches that you can choose to specialize in, depending on your unique proposition:

#1 Life coach/mentor

You will always have that unique experience that someone else doesn't have. Even without a unique experience, you could have a rare vision or perspective that can help someone else.

Traits of a life coach/mentor:

➢ Empathetic
➢ Compassionate

#2 Language tutor

There are over 1000 languages in the world today. The United Nations recognizes over 20 international languages.

Are you proficient in any two international languages? You could easily become a language tutor.

Tutor.com is one prominent platform where you can sell your language skills.

Languageschool.com is another place.

#3 Swimming instructor

Are you good at swimming? Yes, there are many opportunities out there to train people how to swim, especially children.

#4 Music tutor

Music is the language of the heart. If you are good at music, you have a career cut out for you and a business to start.

#5 Art tutor

Are you good at drawing? If you have a talent for drawing, then you can easily train others and earn from it.

#6 Craft tutor

Is there some craft or hobby that you are passionate about? The following are some of the popular crafts: making handicrafts, embroidery, pattern cutting, etc.

#7 Computer app tutor

There are many computer apps. If you know several, especially technical ones such as graphic design apps, movie creation apps, and others, you can easily become a computer tutor for them.

#8 Sports trainer

If you are good at a particular sport, you can add value to your prowess by becoming a trainer in that particular sport. For example, if you are a good basketball player, you can start training kids on how to play basketball.

To be a sports trainer, you do not need to be a professional coach, but you can advance and become a professional. All you need is to share all that you know with those who know very little about your particular sport.

#9 Dance instructor

Dancing is one of the most important physical activities. It is not only for entertainment and socialization, but also for health and fitness. There are rhythmic dances that require significant training to be perfected.

If you dance bolero, salsa, cha-cha, or any other rhythmic dances, you could easily find clients to teach.

#10 Dog trainer

Are you a fan of dogs? Do you know how to train them? There are many people out there who would like their dogs to be trained.

As a dog trainer, you can do it on a freelance basis. People want dogs that can perform in certain ways, or even just need help house-training them.

Content Creation and Publishing

Writing and publishing are about creating and distributing content. You can be a writer (content creator) or a publisher (content distributor) or both.

If you have a unique way with words and people love reading your writing, then you can earn from doing exactly that—writing. Apart from writing, you can also visually demonstrate your content through videos. Blogging and vlogging come into mind.

#11 *Blogger*

Blogging, though not as lucrative as it was in the early days of its inception, can bring you some good income. What matters is that you can write good content that is helpful so that you gain a significant readership and post consistently.

Through blogging, you can become an influencer.

#12 *Vlogger*

Vlogging is just like blogging, but while blogging relies heavily on text, vlogging relies heavily on video content.

Vlogs have overtaken blogs as more people prefer an audiovisual presentation of information.

#13 Content curator

Content curation is about repurposing existing content to suit a particular need. Content curators are especially important when it comes to news media where newsfeeds have to be repurposed to suit the target audience.

#14 Ghostwriter

A ghostwriter is simply a person who writes on behalf of another. Many authors these days hire the services of ghostwriters to write on their behalf. If you find an author with a series of book releases, like a dozen books in a given year, then most likely the author relies on ghostwriters.

#15 Self-publisher

Self-publishing is one step ahead of ghostwriting. In self-publishing, you decide to publish and market your book.

The greatest bottleneck that faces most of the would-be writers is getting their writing approved by publishers. There are many would-be authors whose dreams are quashed at publishing houses.

Thus, if you are confident about your writing, self-publish.

There are several self-publishing platforms such as Amazon Kindle, Barnes and Noble, Google Books, and Kobo, among others.

Chapter 2: Providing Caregiving and Hospitality Services

Caregiving and hospitality are two important personal services that one can render as a business.

Caregiving

#16 Child Care

Child care services include home daycare and babysitting. You can begin with babysitting and after a while graduate to home daycare once you gain experience and become more known.

Some child care services include:

➤ Babysitting

➤ Home daycare

#17 Pet Care

Pet care services include pet-sitting and pet grooming. Sometimes, pet keepers may need to travel to places where they cannot take their pets. This means that they will need someone to pet-sit their beloved animals.

Pet grooming is becoming more common nowadays. Just like personal grooming, pet grooming is becoming big business. Pet grooming includes trimming the pet's fur/hair, brushing the pet's teeth, washing the pet, among others.

#18 Home Care

Home care has many different aspects. Home activities include home cleaning, lawn mowing, upholstery cleaning, home organizing, house-sitting, among others.

Hospitality

#19 Personal assistant(concierge)

Busy executives or people with a busy schedule often require personal assistants (concierges). A personal assistant can provide services such as maintaining a diary, booking appointments, making and responding to calls, taking care of personal errands, among others.

#20 Guest-hosting and ushering

Guest-hosting is common on talk-shows. However, it is not just confined to shows. A guest can come visiting and then you find urgent matters to attend to. This means that you will need someone to do guest-hosting. That is, stand-in for you and entertain your visitors.

Ushering is common during events such as religious services, weddings, and even public events such as public commemorations and others. You can specialize as an usher and liaise with event planners so that you get called whenever there are events.

Eventually, you can incorporate other people and start offering ushering services. This is because there are times when event planners are overwhelmed, especially when more ushers are needed than they can contact or some of the ushers are not available. Letting event planners know that you can have a team of ushers ready makes their work much easier. You provide the team, negotiate the pay, and take charge.

#21 Tour guide and travel agency

You don't need to have visited many places to become a tour guide. You don't need to have taken a tour-guiding course. All you need is to have in-depth knowledge of certain places where people like going. It could be a place within your locality or a place you have visited often and fallen in love with. You take over the planning and guide people to the place.

#22 Catering and food production

Catering services are frequently needed. You can start offering catering services to small gatherings or a few people within your area. Slowly, you can easily expand it as you perfect your skill and business.

Apart from catering services, you can also engage in food production. Some of the foodstuffs that you can make and sell include bread, pastries, cookies, pasta, confections, yogurt, juices, dried vegetables, among others.

#23 Laundry services

In the case where there is free laundry capacity at home (for example, if your home washing machine is not used much) you can offer laundry services within the neighborhood.

#24 Errand services

As people become more and more busy, and as the population ages, there is an increase in door-to-door errands. Some people are either too busy or too old to walk around shopping. Thus, they rely heavily on those who can deliver their shopping and other items to their door.

Check around and see if there is already such a service in your area. Study the demographic and work habits of people within that locality. If most of the households are comprised of either busy working people or old retirees, then there is great potential for you to offer errand services.

It is not only about serving these people, it is also about helping businesses deliver these services. For example, online stores without a physical presence in a given place will rely on errand services to help them deliver products to their customers.

#25 Camping services

Teen camps are common, especially during holidays. Here you can start offering camping services to your fellow teens.

#26 Gift packaging services

During holidays or special events, personalized packaging is often preferred over mechanized packaging. Packaging items such as wine, gourmet foods, gift baskets, etc. can be a great idea.

Chapter 3: Providing Talent-Based Services

The nature of talent-based services is if you have no talent in a particular thing, you cannot fake it. But the great thing about talent-based services is that may discriminate in your favor. All you need is to find that special talent that you have and cultivate a skill around it. Eventually, monetize this skill.

Talent Performance and the Creative Arts

#27 Poetry and spoken word artistry

Spoken word artistry has been gaining ground as a form of talent performance. Spoken word artists are invited to perform at public functions, not only as a form of entertainment but also as a form of public speaking and communication on topical issues.

Just like comedians, singers, and dancers, if you have talent and passion in spoken word artistry, you can make money out of it—not just a wage but also a business. All it needs is to be taken with the seriousness it deserves, just like any other talent-based performance.

#28 Comedy

Comedians are loved. They cause laughter. And as we keep on being reminded, laughter is the medicine of the heart. Comedy is not just entertainment, but also a psychological therapy that can relieve people's stress and depression.

As you crack jokes, crack business too.

#29 Storytelling

Probably one of the oldest forms of performance art, storytelling has existed for ages. With the increasing rate of loneliness, storytelling is picking up as a tool for socialization. Storytellers are invited to inspire people with their stories. Talk-shows are just a spruced-up form of storytelling.

If you have a knack for attracting an audience through your stories, know that you have that talent. Hone it and make it a profession. You can earn a wage from it. And beyond wage, you can make it your business.

#30 Painting

Painting is a talent that begins early in life. It can be refined through practice, though there are still many who discover or focus on this talent late in life.

What is important is that painting is a well-paying talent. And it can be turned into a professional business just like any other, such architecture, engineering, law, etc.

Creative Design

Creative design is not for everyone. If you have talent and passion for artistic work, then this is for you. There is a high demand for creative design work all over the world. The capital needed is quite small. What is needed most is time and creativity.

The following are some of the specialized areas of creative design that you can venture into.

#31 Interior design

You don't have to be a trained professional to be able to become an interior designer. You only need to have design talent and good taste that exhibits class, elegance, and beauty.

#32 Logo design

Businesses require logos. Even your own business requires one. This helps to distinguish your business from millions of others.

You can start working as a logo designer and eventually start a company employing other logo designers, marketers, and other people who will make sure that your business scales up.

#33 Cover page design

Cover page design makes an important impression on books and magazines. It may determine whether someone buys a given book/magazine or not.

Cover page designers are sought worldwide due to their significance in driving sales. If you happen to be one, you have the potential to scale up to a global level and creating not just a job but also a business around your talent and passion.

#34 Graphic design

Graphic design is wide and all-encompassing. It can include computer graphics or hand graphics. Whatever the case, it is one of the most flexible jobs to have as you can do it from any place, any time, provided you have the right facility.

#35 Calligraphy

Calligraphy has largely been overtaken by special computer fonts that mimic handwritten calligraphy. However, the touch of a hand is still revered. Personalized handwriting still stands out. When done artistically by employing calligraphy, then it leaves a more lasting impression.

Organizations still look for those who can write calligraphic messages on their behalf to deliver to their esteemed stakeholders. You can make good money here. Being an art, it is not for everyone. If you are talented, then you can etch your niche and expand beyond it from being a profession to a business.

#36 Fashion design

Fashion never fades. It simply transitions from one form to another. Thus, if you are a fashion designer, you are surrounded by permanent opportunities, as long as you are creative enough to transition with the trends. And if you're the one setting the trend rather than swimming in it, then you become the most-sought leader in this multi-billion dollar borderless industry.

Other Talent-Based Services

#37 Makeup artist

Beauty is eternal. It confounds the notion of time. Everyone wants to appear great. And for the ladies, this is a more pressing need. Thus, if you are talented and skilled in using makeup to make faces appear outstanding, then this is a job that could be full-time and permanent. And if you have an entrepreneurial spirit, there are simply more than enough opportunities to grow your business in this ever-expanding field.

#38 Voice-over artist

Do you have a compelling voice? Voice has become a distinct component of digital marketing and digital products. Those who have a compelling voice are in high demand as voice-over artists.

Products for which voice-over artists are sought are audio books, digital games, digital tutorials, product demos, and many others.

Chapter 4: Providing Skill-Based Services

Any service needs skills for it to be provided. However, there are those services that are by themselves hard skills, meaning that they need hands-on skills where someone is practically using hands or tools to do something, as opposed to simply talking about it.

If you have acquired a skill, either through training or simply observation and practice, you can monetize it to earn a wage or even develop it further into a business.

There are many practical skills that one is endowed with, and also plenty that one can learn. Everyone has some skill. What differs is the monetization. Some skills are in high demand and thus fetch livable wages, while others are in low demand and thus do not fetch livable wages.

Here we are more interested in skills that can bring you a livable wage and which you can develop into a business as an entrepreneur.

Coding and Programming

Without coding and programming, the internet wouldn't exist. As the world switches to digital technology, the demand for software/app programmers goes up.

You can specialize either as a mobile app developer/programmer, web app developer/programmer, or desktop app developer/programmer. The words "developer" and "programmer" are often used interchangeably. However, a programmer is a person who does the coding, while a developer is more of a person who does the business end of it.

#39 Mobile app development

Smartphones are everywhere. People are accessing the internet more on mobile phones than on any other platform. This also means that most digital services require a mobile presence. Mobile apps are the natural means by which these services are accessed. Thus, being a mobile apps developer/programmer opens you up to a world of unlimited opportunities. All you need is to advance your skills and expand your market.

#40 Web app development

Before the advent of smartphones, most digital services were transacted via the web. However, while mobile apps have claimed a giant share of this digital transaction, there are certain sophisticated transactions that still rely heavily on web apps. These include enterprise applications. Being a web app developer is still lucrative and is here to stay for ages to come.

#41 Desktop app development

While desktop apps have largely paved the way for web apps, the demand for desktop apps still exists. Enterprise applications, especially in-house applications, are mostly used on desktops. It is still risky to carry out sensitive enterprise transactions on the web.

#42 Game app development

The digital gaming industry is a multi-billion dollar industry. People of all ages are playing games nowadays. Infotainment has become a new niche that targets adult gamers.

If you have a passion for games and you have good programming skills, you can specialize in developing gaming apps.

#43 Gadget app development

Gadget apps are those that enable the functioning of most gadgets other than smartphones. These gadgets include dongles, IoT devices, robots, drones, etc.

This is an ever-expanding sector where you can find a place for yourself in the long-term.

Repair and Maintenance

If you are a person who likes tinkering with things just to know how they work and fix faulty ones, then repair and maintenance work is right for you.

A lot of repair and maintenance work doesn't require training. It simply requires careful observation, trial-and-error, and experience through practice.

However, there are risky jobs that require training and certification, such as boiler repair, repair of high-voltage electric systems, and such others.

#44 Gadget repair and maintenance

Simple gadgets such as mobile phones, radios, iron boxes, electric cookers, and the like can be easily maintained without the need for advanced technical knowledge. Such maintenance work includes dusting, oiling, etc. Some simple repairs could include replacing burnt fuses and fixing broken electric contacts.

#45 Chimney repair and maintenance

Chimneys require occasional maintenance, which includes removing soot and cleaning. This doesn't require sophisticated skills, but due to busy work schedules, old age, or even allergies, some homeowners may not be able to carry out such easy maintenance work. There is a high demand for this and it's work that you can easily do and make a business out of.

#46 Carpentry and woodwork

Carpentry and woodworking skills can be easily acquired if you have the passion to pursue them. You can earn money making simple household and office furniture such as tables, chairs, stools, cabinets, and shelves. You can also make a business from building office partitions.

#47 Metalwork and blacksmithing

Metalwork and blacksmithing are not for everyone. Make sure that you have no allergies or eye problems. Metalwork and blacksmithing require some apprenticeship training.

Jobs that require welding, metal decor, metal fences, gates, etc. are common. With the appropriate skills, you can venture into this business. You do not need to buy equipment such as a welding machine, you can easily rent it.

#48 Holiday decorating

During the holidays, people want their places to look attractive. This includes homes, offices, businesses, and basically everywhere. It's a time when opportunity knocks for those willing to roll up their sleeves and dive into the holiday atmosphere. Like all holiday sales, this is often temporary.

But, if you plan well in advance to maximize gains when opportunity strikes and invest wisely till the next season of opportunity, this is enough to keep you afloat all year round. You could even contemplate branching out into event and party decoration as well.

#49 Flooring

Oftentimes, flooring becomes necessary not just for aesthetics but also for ease of cleaning and hygiene. And like the occasional change of carpet, there is a need to change floor cover once in a while. If you are skilled in flooring, you just need a few households or offices to breakeven.

If you are a keen observer, flooring is not a complicated skill. It only needs interest and determination, so it takes a short time to learn. There is a high demand for flooring because very few people are willing to dirty their hands doing it, not because it is hard. If you are willing, you've got not just a job, but a potential business to develop.

#50 Parking lot striping

Busy parking lots require striping at least three times a year, and there are plenty of such lots in private facilities as well. If you get a contract to carry out striping for about 10 sizeable parking lots a year, that's significant income. If you are entrepreneurial enough, this is a starting point to make it a business that can easily scale up.

Beauty and Cosmetics

The beauty and cosmetics industry is evergreen. There could be some slightly low seasons, but it remains upbeat throughout the year, with sudden peaks during holidays or important events.

#51 Instant shaving and massage

Busy people don't have the time to visit shaving and massage parlors. Taking such services to where they spend most of their time is the best way to meet their needs.

You don't need much to have good shaving and massage tools. What is required are skills and a go-getter spirit.

#52 Hairstylist

Being a hairstylist is a lucrative business. Many busy professionals have hairstylists who work for them just as personal assistants do. Thus, if you attend high-end clients, you can become their hairstylist.

You can also have a portable barbershop where you can render door-to-door barber and styling services.

#53 Fashion modeling

Fashion houses and beauty products require models to induce demand and push their sales. If you have the natural features and the subtle mien required, then this is a great job for you. It is a job that you can use to easily scale up once you become a successful professional.

Miscellaneous Skills

#54 Personal chef

If you love cooking, being a personal chef can be such a great job. When cooking is a natural part of you, then it isn't difficult to perfect your culinary art. It all needs practice. Some are trained, yet don't do well simply because it is not their natural talent or they lack the requisite passion for it. But it demands passion and the will to experiment. Start offering your services part-time during events as a chef and once you gain confidence, boldly seek out opportunities. Culinary skills don't require a certain minimum age, it is all a matter of how skilled you are and how passionate you go about it. The only age limit could be about becoming formally employed, but begin with close family members. The close circle is the best way to begin as a teen.

#55 Photographer

The big thing about photography is that it is just as much about passion and artistic vision as skill. Some kids are doing photography and have not even become teens. So as a teen, you can do it.

The big thing with photography is that age is not a real factor. Thus, if you are capable of doing it and have a passion for it, that's it. All you need is a good camera. Cameras are cheap, but even if certain work requires sophisticated photography, it isn't that expensive to rent one. Try capturing unique photos and selling them on photo sites (Getty, etc.).

#56 Secretary

Secretarial services include report writing, taking minutes, booking appointments, updating diaries, scheduling meetings, etc.

It also includes transcription work, typing, and such other services.

#57 Virtual Assistant

A virtual assistant is a person who renders secretarial, reception, and/or administrative services over the internet. This person is not physically available within the premises of the client.

With more businesses turning to e-commerce modes of operation, and with physical offices become more expensive in terms of rent, virtual services have picked up. Working remotely is the future of employment.

You can work as a virtual assistant and with proper organizational skills, you can establish your call center from your living room or study and hire a few people to assist you.

#58 Bookkeeper

Learning bookkeeping is a short-term course of about six-months, and is enough to help you get started. Afterwards, you can gradually advance as you work. With cloud computing software, many businesses are preferring to have their records in the cloud. This means you can render bookkeeping services from the convenience of your study, room, or couch. All you need is a laptop/desktop plus steady internet.

#59 Language translator

Are you good at languages? If you have a passion for languages and know at least two international languages, then you are already in business. All you need is to get started, especially if you know English and a bit of another language. Many people and businesses would like their content to be translated into English.

Chapter 5: Providing Consultancy Services

Contrary to what many believe, you don't need to have a college degree to become a consultant. What you need to become a consultant is simply expert knowledge within a certain niche.

#60 Social media consultant

Being a social media consultant requires you to be able to advise clients on how best to effectively utilize social media to achieve their objectives.

There is no special course required for this. Having in-depth experience with a given social media such as Instagram, Snapchat, Twitter, or Facebook is all you need. The only issue is that you must have reached the required age: at least 16 years for U.S. citizens.

#61 Design consultant

Being a design consultant doesn't require a minimum age, what it requires is special expertise in your respective field.

Some of the areas where you can practice as a design consultant include interior design, landscape design, outdoor spaces, etc. Other niches include toy design, game design, and furniture design.

#62 Music consultant

You can carry out coaching services in your area of expertise. This is not age-dependent, as long as you have the right expertise.

For example, you can become a piano coach even before becoming an adult. Most music skills such as coaching people how to play the violin, bass guitar, keyboard, etc. do not require you to be of age.

If you are talented in art, you can also coach people how to draw.

#63 Event consultant

Events and parties take place for all ages. As a teen, you can organize events/parties for fellow teens such as birthday parties, graduation parties, and others. You can easily start by planning events/parties for your younger siblings or relatives and family friends. Gradually, you will be able to host bigger events as you expand your circle of influence.

Chapter 6: Cottage Industrialist

"Cottage industry" simply refers to the small-scale, home-based industry. Cottage industries have been the incubator of rapid industrialization and the prototype for small-scale manufacturing.

You are not too young to become an industrialist: you can start right at home as a cottage industrialist.

Making and Selling DIY Craftwork

#64 DIY jewelry and ornaments

You don't have to buy precious metals to make jewelry and ornaments. What matters is how attractive and unique your piece of jewelry or ornament is. You can make beautiful jewelry from beads, porcelain, bones, ceramics, seeds, and other materials.

You can also make ornamental frames for doors, windows, mirrors, photographs, and portraits.

#65 DIY electronic gadgets

There are plenty of DIY kits that you can develop further into electronic gadgets such as IoT gadgets, robotic toys, small drones, and others. These kits include Arduino, Raspberry PI, Adafruit, Beaglebone, etc.

To be able to derive a market from your DIY electronic gadgets, target functional items. That is, items that can serve a useful purpose.

#66 DIY tailoring and dressmaking

Tailoring is an easy business to start. A simple sewing machine will cost you less than $40. Furthermore, there is plenty of idle capacity in many tailoring businesses and you can agree with the owner to borrow or rent the machine on a part-time basis as need be.

#67 DIY embroidery

Embroidery is a great textile art that is appreciated by many art lovers. While print designs have taken much of the market that was hitherto the domain of embroidery, this has resulted in a more refined artistic niche.

Just like designer clothes have their premium niche market, embroidery also has its niche market—for those who appreciate its sheer beauty and are willing to pay for it.

For a beginner like you who is on a $100 shoestring budget, the best way to start is to focus on hand-made embroidery where all you need are a special set of needles plus an assortment of strings. In total, they won't cost more than $20. You can start with cheap material for small items such as face towels, stool covers, pillow covers, etc. This way, the cost of the material will be low. You can move on with spending a maximum of $30 on materials, such as the fabric and the frames. You are left with about $50: you can spend $30 on marketing and save the $20 for future use.

#68 DIY weaving and basketry

With many countries banning plastic bags due to environmental concerns, basketry is regaining lost ground.

If you are a skilled weaver, basketry is the best place to start your weaving business. You can time your basketry work to coincide with the gift-giving season so that you can pitch your baskets as gift baskets.

Just like embroidery, basketry doesn't have to cost much. The budgetary range is the same.

#69 DIY Leatherwork

Leatherwork pays. You can make special leather designs such as leather shoes, sandals, jackets, wallets, bags, etc.

You can create your label and market both locally and online. Amazon, eBay, and Etsy, are just a few of the marketplaces where you can get your products sold. You can also target fashion houses.

#70 DIY metalwork and fabrication

Metalwork and fabrication don't require expensive tools to get started. With $50 you can get most of the basic tools that you need. You can reserve the rest for materials and other needs. Expensive tools are not needed as they will lie idle most of the time. It is actually more economical to rent them than to buy them.

When it comes to materials, you can cut costs by starting with light metalwork as you build up your enterprise. Even if you get a bigger project, you can create a joint venture with those who have enough resources to execute it.

Being portable and available at small construction sites can land you some small jobs that will keep you going as you improve your skills and establish your market.

You can also engage in decorative metalwork as a hobby during your free time. This can induce demand even for those within your neighborhood. For example, decorative handles, decorative curtain rods, decorative flower pot stands, and other small items.

#71 DIY pottery and claywork

Pottery and claywork are not common nowadays, but if you are in a rural setup where you can get clay, then you can be able to make pots for sale. Some love clay pots for their growing flowers. Alternatively, you can use a special cement to achieve the same.

Only consider this if you have a passion for it and the raw materials are available within your area. Flower vendors are potential customers to pursue.

#72 DIY carvings, sculptures, and molds

Carvings and sculptures are a form of artistic craftwork. Some of these are based on:

➤ Wood carvings
➤ Soapstone carvings
➤ Bone carvings
➤ Solid wax for mold and sculpting

Statues are the commonest types of carvings and sculptures and there is a great market for wood carvings and sculptures. eBay is one of the popular marketplaces to sell them.

The raw materials are quite cheap, especially for small carvings. You can get special wood for about $30 apiece. Soapstone is relatively cheaper than wood where it is available.

Apart from carving and sculpting, molding is another way you can display artistic craftwork. All you need is a malleable material and the cast. Wax is the commonest material used for molding artistic impressions. You can advance your artistry by using a 3D printer once you are well-established and can afford to buy one. But even without buying, you can still rent.

Making and Selling DIY Healthcare and Therapeutic Products

#73 DIY natural skincare products, natural cosmetics

The demand for pharmaceutical-free natural cosmetics is skyrocketing. Many people are scared of pharmaceutical cosmetics that make them look great for a short while but leave them with long-term or permanent skin damage.

You can easily learn how to prepare DIY natural cosmetics. It isn't very complicated and the rewards can be great.

#74 DIY laundry and hygiene products

Laundry and hygiene products are some of the simplest products that you can make from home. All you need is to follow the prescribed formula. Materials are also easily and cheaply available. However, depending on your jurisdiction, you may need to have a production license.

The following are some of the laundry and hygiene products that you can easily make:

➢ Laundry soaps
➢ Detergents
➢ Herbal soaps
➢ Hand sanitizers

PART II: LEASING AND RENTALS BUSINESSES

Leasing and rentals are about properties, which are quite expensive to buy. But not all of them are, and some tools and equipment can be within your affordability range as a teenager.

The most important thing to note is that you don't have to own any property to engage in the business of leasing and renting. Real estate agents don't own the properties they lease and rent.

If your parents have some property that is lying idle, this is your opportunity to make charity begin at home. Use the power of persuasion to allow you start the leasing and renting business.

And if your parents are pretty hard nuts to crack, package yourself as a broker/agent. Use a few dollars to print those business cards and start convincing property owners that you can help them find customers for their rentals. Build a list of potential customers and create a strategy to become that middle link.

There are many things to do in this business. You don't have to start with expensive property, there is a lot within your reach. Here we'll show you a lot more that's attainable and what you can do with it.

Chapter 7: Leasing Items

There are compelling reasons that make it more reasonable to lease an item instead of buying it. Some of these reasons include:

- ➢ Cost factors. Capital items can be expensive to buy. It's cheaper to lease.
- ➢ Limited use. If you are going to use a tool or equipment or space just once or occasionally, then it doesn't make sense to buy it and let it lie idle.

There are so many items that can be rented out. This makes it a business opportunity to consider. You can lease tools and equipment, books, furniture, tents and camping facilities, among so many others. Just look around and think of what you can rent out at a fee.

#75 Leasing tools and equipment

Buying tools and leasing them can be a lucrative business. You only need to start small, but then aim higher.

You can buy used or second-hand tools and equipment and then rent them. If you don't have that much money to buy the tools or equipment, you can simply rent them and then lease them out for a higher rate. What you need is to have your ear to the ground, that means knowing the suppliers and looking out for customers.

Some of the tools that you can rent out include:
- ➢ Welding tools
- ➢ Battery chargers
- ➢ Drainage water pumps
- ➢ Drilling tools
- ➢ Power saw

#76 Leasing books (lending library)

Establishing a lending library is easy. You can begin with the books that you no longer use. You can also ask friends to add to your library and offer the books that they don't use for a small fee or in exchange with those from their friends. The main goal is to create a pool of books.

You can advertise your lending business on social media such as Twitter, Snapchat, etc. You can also create a free blog using blogger.com or wordpress.com where you can update your clients about your collections and additions.

#77 Leasing furniture and catering equipment

Generally, buying furniture is out of the reach of the $100 budget. However, that doesn't stop you from renting out furniture. You can rent and lease furniture, and gain the differential margin as your profit. For example, if you hire a given piece of furniture at $3 a day and lease it out at $5, you'll be able to gain a margin of $2 per piece of furniture.

People hire furniture for events since there is no need to buy and keep what they will rarely be using. For them, it is more economical to rent than buy. Furthermore, some functions will require a lot more furniture than they can afford to buy at once, so it makes much more sense to rent. Some of the furniture that people mostly rent include chairs, tables, etc.

Apart from furniture, people also hire catering equipment during functions such as weddings, parties, and picnics. Some of the commonly hired catering equipment include food warmers, water dispensers, plates, etc. Like furniture, you can also hire and lease out catering equipment.

#78 Leasing tents and outdoor equipment

Tents and outdoor equipment are usually in high demand during the summer months or in places where the weather is fairly warm.

Both tents and most outdoor equipment are out of your $100 budget. But you can afford to hire and rent out such that 50% of your budget goes to marketing while the remainder can be saved for emergencies.

#79 Leasing vehicles

Unless your parents or friends are willing to lend you their car, or you already have one, a $100 budget is out of your purchase power. What you can do is to hire the car and rent it out.

To maximize on returns or to make the deal more attractive, if you are of driving age within your jurisdiction (mostly, above 16 years old), you can offer chauffeur services for those ready to hire a car from you.

Chapter 8: Leasing Free Space

Developed space is becoming scarce and more expensive. People are looking for free space that they can rent for a short while.

Some of the functions that give rise to short leases include parking, short meetings, guest rest places, picnics, entertainment spots, photographic or cinematographic scenery, among others.

Location matters. It is important to consider if your location is ideal for what you want to lease it out for. Some locations are ideal for certain things while not ideal for others.

Find out the unique thing that your location is ideal for and create a market for it. Sometimes you have to induce demand by informing people of what you think your space could do.

#80 Leasing your parents' garage

If your parents have free garage space and they don't mind you leasing it out, grab that opportunity.

Think of what that garage could be used for. If it is near the main road, it could be a place for several things. It could be a temporary parking lot, an exhibition spot for merchandise or artwork, a tented meeting place, etc.

If it is a bit far away from the main road, it could be a hideout for those who seek privacy. It could host small private parties.

#81 Leasing part of your house/room

Co-living has become common nowadays. Young people lease places to share not because they cannot afford to live alone, but simply because they need a place where they can have company.

If your parents accept it, you can talk to friends about co-living opportunities. They can tell others about it. Don't lease out a part of your house/room to strangers. It must be someone you know well, or someone known to your close friend or relative.

Also, attics and penthouses are great places to just relax and spend time. This is especially the case if they are overlooking some beautiful scenery.

If your parent's attic or penthouse overlooks a great view such as mountains, lakes, a canopy, or some beautiful landscape, this can be a great place for those seeking change.

You can pitch that great scene and market the attic or penthouse. There will be interest. Take great photos showing the scenic beauty from the vantage position within the penthouse or attic.

This can be a great place for a romantic outing.

#82 Leasing meeting space

Meeting in restaurants or conference halls can be very expensive, especially for small routine meetings. A lot of people prefer a place where they can pay on an hourly basis and just have a basic arrangement.

The meeting space can be in a garage, extra room (in case your brother or sister has moved away), and even the living room when your parents plan to be away for a while.

#83 Renting space and leasing it out

In case it is not possible to use your parents' premises, you can rent a space and lease it out. However, this requires some great marketing skills.

For example, you can rent a meeting room for a whole day and lease it out on an hourly basis. This way, you canearn extra since the rate for hourly meetings is higher per hour compared to the rate for daily renting.

PART III: TRADING BUSINESSES

Trading businesses are about the buying and selling of goods. This is by far the commonest form of business.

The greatest challenge facing teens when it comes to trading businesses is the stocking cost. However, as we shall discover, you do not always have to keep stock to trade. There are smart ways of avoiding stock costs and even avoiding hiring a shop, since rent is also out of reach for many.

Discover more on how you can trade without your capital being tied to stock and rent.

Chapter 9: Personal Sales and Marketing

Personal sales refers to promoting a product through a face-to-face encounter to close a sale. The following are some of the products that you can transact through personal sales:

➤ Merchandise

➤ Services

➤ Ideas

➤ Influence

#84 Personal sales of merchandise

Merchandise refers to physical products. This is by far the commonest form of trade. While selling at a shop is largely personal selling, for this context we designate the personal selling of merchandize as the kind of sales whereby the seller deliberately uses personal contact or relationships to drive sales.

Unlike in an ordinary shop where the shopkeeper waits for someone to walk in; in personal sales, the seller makes the effort of reaching out to the customer through rapport and influence. Examples of personal sales of merchandise include going door-to-door.

#85 Personal sales of services

Apart from the merchandise, service ranks as the second most common product that is transacted through personal sales. Certain products are more attuned to personal sales than others, such as insurance policies and loans.

#86 Personal sales of ideas

Idea sales refers to being able to influence people so that they buy into your idea. That is, causing them to take a profitable action through your influence.

#87 Personal sales of influence

Influence marketing refers to leveraging your leadership influence to induce a sale. People who have huge followings, such as musicians and sports figures, are often used to promote products and drive sales. As such, they are not selling the merchandize but rather, they are selling their influence to merchandisers.

#88 Influencer marketing

Influencer marketing is a specialized form of the personal sale of ideas. In this case, the influencer endorses a given product or service without directly pitching sales. As such, it is a form of indirect personal selling.

The influencer marketer hopes that their followers will also do as the influencer does; that is, use the product/service that the influencer uses.

Influencer marketing has gained prominence with the advent of social media. It is the most impactful component of social media marketing.

#89 Network marketing

Network marketing is a great method of personal sales. However, it is one of the most abused means of marketing and has gained a bad reputation. Nonetheless, for reputable products, it is still a great way to conduct personal sales. A big advantage of network marketing is the ability to quickly scale up.

#90 Affiliate marketing

Affiliate marketing is a form of personal sales whereby you earn a certain commission based on the people you successfully introduce to a given product or service. The commission could be based on a successful sale or simply a successful introduction.

Even though affiliate marketing can be done traditionally, it is the most common form of online marketing. This dual purpose makes it great for brick-and-mortar enterprises with an online presence.

Chapter 10: Selling Products Online

#92 Private labeling and fulfillment

Private labeling

Labeling refers to uniquely branding an item. Private labeling means uniquely branding an already existing product so that it appears as a unique product from you. For example, you can buy a plain T-shirt from a supplier and brand your name or logo on it. This becomes your private label of the T-shirt.

Fulfillment

The term "fulfillment" is commonly used in the merchandise business by vendors when it comes to dealing with orders. The order is either "fulfilled" or "unfulfilled." A fulfilled order is one where the goods are delivered as per the order and all its terms are met, including invoicing, billing and payment. An unfulfilled order is an order that has not yet been acted upon or is not completed.

Thus, in a more technical sense, fulfillment can be defined as the whole process of receiving, packaging and delivering the order.

Fulfillment is commonly applied in e-commerce as well on sites such as Amazon FBA, Airbnb, etc.

#92 Dropshipping

Dropshipping is a type of retail fulfillment whereby the retailers don't keep the stock of the products they are selling. Instead, they deliver the products directly from wholesalers to consumers.

Because you are not handling stock, the cost of stocking and delivery is off your shoulders. All you need is your e-commerce website and an appropriate dropshipping app.

Starting your dropshipping site is easy with Shopify and the monthly fee is only $29. You can also get free themes for your storefront or buy custom ones cheaply ($20 or less) from the Shopify marketplace. Once you have your Shopify site running, install the Orbelo plugin for dropshipping. Once Orbelo is installed, you can visit places like Aliexpress and order products that can be delivered to your customer, per their order. With Orbelo, this is automated.

#93 Online retail arbitrage

"Buy Low, Sell High" is what arbitrage is all about. Retail arbitrage is about buying products at a lower price in one marketplace and selling them at a higher price in another marketplace.

When you don't have much money to trade with, you can take advantage of online retail arbitrage by listing items on one marketplace that are discounted on another marketplace.

For example, if item X is priced at $10 on Amazon and is being sold at a 25% discount on eBay, you can list the very same item on Amazon at $10 with a 10% discount. Your discount offer is to attract quick sale and outcompete others. Your margin of profit will be the difference in the discount rate (that is, 25%-10% = 15%). Once the customer places an order for your product on Amazon, you can quickly place an order for the same item on eBay.

In this case, you have not spent a coin of your own money. You have simply taken advantage of the price differential.

With time, you can even create your own e-commerce shop and list the items on your site, in addition to other marketplaces.

#94 Buying and selling used items and antiques

Selling used items and antiques is a profitable niche. This is because, unlike new products where customers can easily make a comparison, there is no comparison for used products. Thus, the profit margin is highly elastic.

Some of the lucrative items to venture into include:

➢ Buying and selling used books
➢ Buying and selling used apparel
➢ Buying and selling used boots

#95 Selling digital products and services

There is an increasing preference for digital products and services due to their easy access and affordability. For less than $50 of initial capital, you can easily start any of the following digital business:

➤ Buying and selling software apps
➤ Buying and selling domains
➤ Website flipping
➤ Offering hosting services

#96 Sourcing and outsourcing services

Sourcing and outsourcing is a kind of business whereby you specialize in finding products or services for business needs, buy them, and then resell them to those who need them at a markup.

The most important thing in this business is first-hand information. First of all, you compile two lists. The first list is of services/products in demand and those who need them. The second list is of those who provide the services or sell the products that are in demand.

With a proper strategy, you can conduct this business without incurring any production or stock related costs. For example, you can arrange it so that those who want to source the service make a downpayment and those who source the product pay an order or make a deposit. For those who are providing the service, you pay them sometime after the service is fully delivered. And for those who provide physical goods, you negotiate for a longer credit period, e.g. 30 days. Thus, you have sufficient time to make sure that the transaction is settled without incurring any production or stocking costs.

#97 E-commerce technopreneur

Many e-commerce platforms only require installation and customization. It's very easy to do and doesn't require any advanced programming to learn how to install and customize these platforms. WooCommerce is one such easy e-commerce platform if you know how to install and run WordPress. Shopify is another easy one. Even with advanced e-commerce platforms such as Magento and PrestaShop, you won't spend more than $30 if you decide to outsource installation and customization.

So you can easily become an e-commerce technopreneur. The following are some of the things that you can achieve:

➢ Building and selling ready-made e-commerce shops
➢ Creating and optimizing e-commerce listings (e.g. on Airbnb, Amazon, eBay, Etsy, etc.)
➢ Installing and customizing e-commerce platforms on behalf of clients

PART IV: MICRO-FARMING

While farming is generally preferred in rural areas, rapid and expansive urbanization has meant that relying on rural areas alone is not enough. Furthermore, due to high transportation, storage, and preservation costs (including health costs), many urban dwellers have considered micro-farming as a way of supplementing their daily diet and even making some income out of it.

Gone are the days when farming used to be just a rural enterprise and when micro-farming used to be considered as an activity for grandparents. Farming can also be an urban enterprise and teens are engaging in micro-farming not just as a hobby, but also as an income activity. Some have even extended this into a business activity.

In this section, I'll show you some of the micro-farming activities that you can carry out in a limited space and on less than a $100 budget.

Chapter 11: Organic Farming

As people continue to discover the adverse effects of chemical fertilizers, pesticides, and preservatives, the more they become inclined towards organic foods.

Globally, there is an increase in demand for organic foods. In the United States, organically grown foods continue to fetch higher prices than non-organically grown foods. This brings great rewards to organic farmers.

Being a teen, this is an excellent opportunity. You don't need to buy a farm to do so. There are certain high-paying plant sources of organic foods that you can grow on a micro-scale. Herbs, mushrooms, and others are easy to start with less than a $100 budget.

#98 Herb farming

The use of herbs is quite versatile. Some herbs are used for therapeutic purposes, others are used for culinary purposes, and yet others are used for aromatic purposes.

The greatest advantage of herbs is that you don't need tons of acres to farm them, just a small space is enough. Spaces you can use for herb farming:

➤ Kitchen garden

- ➢ Attic space
- ➢ Veranda space
- ➢ Walkway
- ➢ Special room

Common herbs that you can grow:

- ➢ Rosemary
- ➢ Octavia
- ➢ Coriander
- ➢ Ginger

#99 Mushroom farming

Mushrooms are extremely delicious. They are also rich in nutrients, especially essential minerals. However, finding natural habitats for their growth is becoming increasingly rare due to inorganic fertilizer pollution and high-tech farm mechanization.

However, the good thing about mushrooms is that they don't need much to grow. Only a good substrate and some shelves, plus good room temperature and lighting.

A great thing about mushroom farming is that you can optimize free space that would have otherwise been wasted.

Spaces you can use for mushroom farming:

- ➢ Attic space
- ➢ Basement
- ➢ Special room

Chapter 12: Tech Farming

Tech farming refers to the kind of farming that involves widescale use of technology so that plants can grow naturally within the space, environment, and conditions in which they are placed, enabling them to grow, flourish and produce.

Some technologies are more sophisticated than others and more capital intensive than others.

Let's look at technologies that you can implement on a simple budget of $100 or less. These include:

#100 Hydroponic gardening

Hydroponics is a modern way of raising plants without the need to use soil. It heavily relies on the use of water and non-soil mediums to grow.

Why hydroponics? Hydroponics has increased in popularity of late. People engage in mini-farming for various reasons, but the following are some of the main ones:

➤ To lower food budgets
➤ To have guaranteed fresh produce
➤ To utilize free land
➤ To keep oneself physically active
➤ To practice as a hobby
➤ To earn some extra income

#101 Aquaponic gardening

Aquaponic gardening is a way of raising fish and plants together in a mechanism that does not use soil for plants.

The following are the main differences between hydroponics and aquaponics:

➢ Hydroponics is about monoculture (growing plants alone) while aquaponics is about mixed culture (both plants and livestock).

➢ You can use inorganic fertilizer in hydroponics while you need to use organic fertilizer in aquaponics. This is because inorganic fertilizer could be dangerous to fish.

➢ Aquaponic troughs need to be deeper than hydroponic troughs because fish need more space to maneuver.

➢ Generally, aquaponic farming is much more sensitive to environmental conditions and thus requires more delicate care than hydroponics. This is because some factors that may be good for plants may not necessarily be good for the fish and vice versa. You have to be sensitive to both needs.

➢ You can more easily meet your household dietary requirements with aquaponics than with hydroponics. This is because there is an animal protein source (fish) when it comes to aquaponics, which hydroponics lacks.

#102 Container gardening

Container gardening is one of the easiest and oldest forms of tech farming. It simply means that you plant your crops into a container. The container can be a:

➢ Pot

➢ Jerrycan

➢ Old tire

➢ Gunnysack

➢ Plastic soda bottle

Plants that can grow in containers can be herbs such as:

➢ Parsley

➢ Mint

➢ Oregano

➢ Basil

➢ Rosemary

➢ Chives

➢ Bay

➢ Thyme

➢ Basil

➢ Sorrel

➢ Lemon balm

Also, vegetables such as:

➢ Eggplant

➢ Carrots

➢ Kale

➢ Tomatoes

Chapter 13: Raising Livestock

Livestock farming is not just limited to rural areas. If you are in a rural area, that's great for you. Farming is already a major activity there and it is easy to get started. However, if you are in an urban setup, this becomes a challenge. Yet the challenge isn't insurmountable. It simply means that you get to choose which breeds to keep and which ones not to.

We are going to consider livestock that you can raise on a micro-farm. That is, within a small space characteristic of a typical urban residence. However, this does not necessarily mean that if you are in a rural setup then you cannot do micro-farming. As a teen, your parents will probably only allocate very small space for you to start. So even in a rural setup, you are more likely to start as a micro-farmer.

#103 Raising pets for sale

Most people love pets. Dogs and cats are some of the most sought after pets. You can easily start a pet business with $0 capital.

The following are the ways in which you can get your pet at $0 initial capital:

- ➢ Donation of a puppy or kitten by a family member, friend, or neighbor. People donate pets when they are beyond their capacity to keep them, when they are relocating, or the pet owner is deceased.
- ➢ Getting a pet from an animal rescue center. When the owner of a stray cannot be traced, then the pet is offered for free to those who are ready to keep it. Another case is when the pet owner abuses the pet so it gets rescued. Lastly, owners of a pet can take it to an animal rescue center if they no longer wish to keep it.

In case you do cannot get a pet for free, then, you will need to buy it. The best way to buy a pet cheaply is to buy a very young pet.

Make sure that your pet is immunized immediately when you receive it.

Other than dogs and cats, other pets include:

- ➢ Birds – such as peacocks, guinea hens, pigeons, doves, etc.
- ➢ Reptiles – such as snakes (non-venomous), lizards, chameleons, etc.
- ➢ Amphibians – such as frogs, etc.
- ➢ Rabbits and rodents– such as mice, rats, hamsters, guinea pigs, etc.

#104 Raising birds for sale

Apart from being raised as pets, birds can be raised either for eggs or meat. On rare occasions, some birds can be raised for their feathers.

Common types of birds raised for eggs and meat include:

➢ Chickens

➢ Ducks

➢ Guinea hens

➢ Turkeys

You can start by raising chickens for sale since there is an easy market. However, as you advance, you may consider ducks and turkeys since, unlike chickens, they are less susceptible to diseases and have higher survival rates.

To start your bird raising business, buy young chicks (e.g. seven days old) and feed them to maturity. Also, start with breeding for eggs and then later on venture into breeding for meat. This is because eggs are easier to sell than meat.

Chapter 14: Ornamental Farming

Ornamental farming is about raising livestock and growing plants for ornamental purposes—simply for their beauty and attractiveness.

It is common to see ornamental plants in urban residential areas and even offices. Some palatial homes even have ornamental livestock such as ornamental birds, reptiles, and dogs.

#105 Growing flowers for sale (floriculture)

Flowers are largely ornamental plants. They are bought and kept for their aesthetic value.

If you are in urban areas, you can plant and sell potted plants, while in rural areas, you can plant and sell carnations, in addition to potted plants.

However, with tech farming, you can still plant and sell carnations using a greenhouse combined with hydroponics.

#106 Growing bonsai trees for sale

Bonsai trees are short shrub-like trees. Bonsai technology can dwarf certain species of large trees and make them grow as short as less than one foot.

Due to their size, bonsai trees can be kept both indoors and outdoors. One can have a beautiful bonsai garden that mimics a natural forest.

Planting and selling bonsai is a lucrative business, yet it does not require much money to start out. It could take as low as under $30 to get started. What is important is to have the knowledge and skill of the bonsai species and how to grow them.

#107 Raising ornamental fish for sale

Ornamental fish are often raised in an aquarium. Sometimes the aquarium can be as tiny as a portable bottle for the tiny species.

The great thing about the ornamental fish business is that, in most cases, the customers that you sell the fish to may request that you to take up the job of caring for them. So other than the business itself, you may be able to leverage a job out of it, killing two birds with one stone.

For a small aquarium, the entire investment can cost $30. The best way to optimize returns out of your $100 budget is to have one aquarium for demo purposes and get jobs based on a Cash-With-Order (CWO) basis. CWO ensures that you do not trap your little cash into the investment and it is the customers who fund your project.

#108 Raising ornamental birds for sale

Ornamental birds are mostly raised due to their beautiful feathers. Some are raised due to their tiny size. A few are raised due to their unique sound.

A great idea is to have a bonsai landscape in a sizeable cage with two to three beautiful tiny birds in it. However, this may cost slightly more than $100. You can start by selling the birds in a cage, but advertise the bigger project for those willing to pay upfront (Cash-With-Order).

A DIY cage can cost you about $15 or less. You can buy a tiny bird for $20 or less. Having two samples for a start is a great way to begin.

#109 Raising ornamental reptiles for sale

The chameleon is one of the most beloved ornamental reptiles. This is due to its changing colors that suit its environment while camouflaging itself. Chameleons also are less costly to maintain and are not aggressive, so they don't require a lot of attention or risk-proof enclosures.

If you visit their habitats in the wild, it is easy to get a chameleon for free. Have a breathable container to keep it in and take it home. Before this, prepare an enclosure garden for it and its meal—mainly flies. It could take less than $30 for the entire arrangement if you get a chameleon for free. Keep several for the sake of mating and breeding so that you can create a business out of it.

#110 Raising ornamental insects for sale

Butterflies are the most popular ornamental insects. This is due to their beautiful and highly attractive colors. Another great advantage of butterflies is that they don't cost much to raise. You can easily get butterflies for free if they happen to be in your area. All you need is a small garden enclosure with flowers inside. Cultivate flowers that have nectar. You can also smear sugar onto some dry twigs for them to lick.

#111 Growing ornamental herbs for sale

Ornamental herbs are those herbs that are grown for aesthetic purpose. That is, the provide improved appearance of the surroundings.

The following are main types of ornamental herbs:

➤ Herbs that provide blossoming ambience, e.g. Garlic chives, Thyme, Rosemary, Dittany, and Catmint.

- Herbs that provide aromatic fragrance, e.g. Chamaemelum nobile, Australian mint bush, and Lavender.
- Herbs that attract beautiful insects such as butterflies, e.g. Chamomile, and Jacob's ladder.
- Herbs that attract beautiful birds, e.g. Angelica, Borage, Lavender, Sage, and Valerian.
- Herbs that attract humming bees, e.g. Borage, and Tutti Frutti.
- Herbs whose branches and canopy provides scenic beauty.
- Herbs that repel unwanted insects (such as mosquitoes, and ants), and rodents (such as mice) e.g. Sage (mosquito repellant), Lemongrass (mosquito repellant), and creeping pennyroyal (ants and mice repellant).
- Herbs that provides hedge, e.g. Salem Rosemary, Echinacea, Angelica, and Hedge germander.

PART V: TIPS THAT WILL GROW YOUR $100

The greatest challenge facing teens is how to make sure that their little capital goes a long way in growing their business.

With careful planning, keen attention, and sheer cleverness, $100 can easily push your business to higher growth momentum.

In this section, I'll provide you with tips that can help you optimize your $100 budget so that it grows instead of fizzling out.

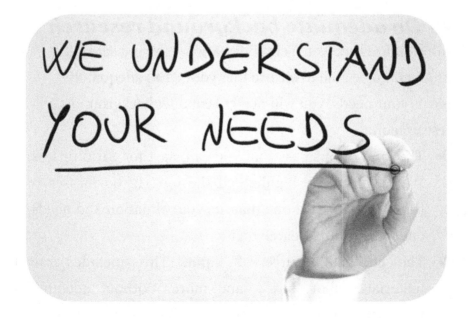

Chapter 15: Tips for Working on a $100 Shoestring Budget

Working on a shoestring budget of $100 or less requires that you be careful with your cashflow. Cash management is paramount, so you must limit your cash expenditure as much as possible. Whenever you can, you'll need to substitute cash with non-cash equivalents.

The following are some of the tips that will make your $100 go far and make your dream micro-enterprise a reality.

#1 Do adequate background research

Information is power. Yet, information itself is a saleable product. To be able to ensure that your $100 adequately meets your needs, you will need to conduct background research on:

➤ The kind of business that you can start for $100 or less. We have already highlighted the top 112 businesses to think about. Select one that fits your situation and needs, and focus your research on it.

➤ The cheapest source of input. This includes raw materials, labor, space, and more. Without adequate research, you may end up incurring a higher cost for input that you could have gotten cheaper elsewhere. Don't be surprised to find yourself saving even up to 80% of your input cost thanks to thorough research.

Treat information as your most important asset and research as your most important tool.

#2 Plan and budget ahead

If you fail to plan, then you have simply planned to fail. The smaller the amount you have at your disposal, the more precise your planning and budgeting ought to be. The value of $1 out of $100 is more than the value of $10 out of $1000. Every cent should count.

Plan so that every resource and every effort is utilized most economically. Budget so that every sacrifice achieves the highest possible gain and, if possible, at the lowest possible cost.

#3 Minimize fixed costs

Fixed costs are those costs that don't depend on your level of activity or output. You incur them whether your output is high or low. On the other hand, the variable cost depends on your activity or output. With variable cost, it simply means that zero output equals zero cost.

Fixed costs include rent, salary, etc. You can minimize the fixed component of a cost by incurring it at the lowest unit possible. For example, when it comes to renting, you can pay per hour or foot. This makes it adjustable. When it comes to labor, instead of paying a monthly salary, pay an hourly wage.

#4 Rent instead of buy

When you are starting out, you aren't sure how your business will go. Instead of spending money to buy expensive equipment, simply rent it whenever possible. Alternatively, you can also try to borrow.

Only when the business picks up and you consider it more economical in the long-run to buy than to rent, then you can make purchasing decisions.

#5 Avoid idle capacity

Idle capacity means inefficiency. Idle capacity could take the form of empty space, equipment that is not being used, laborers who are not assigned duties, and resources that are not being utilized.

To avoid idle capacity:

➤ Rent facilities only when you are able and ready to utilize them.

➤ Sublease the facility under hire but not in immediate use.

#6 Boost productivity and economy

Productivity is about getting the most optimal output per given input. On the other hand, economy is about utilizing resources more effectively and efficiently.

When you start small, every dollar counts, and every extra unit of output per given resource counts too. Thus, if you have to maximize returns from your $100 and increase wealth, you must boost productivity and economy.

#7 Substitute wage with non-cash rewards

You can afford to work on your enterprise without a wage, but you cannot expect a free helping hand. Labor is expensive and can easily exhaust your $100 within a few hours.

If you need extra hands to work for you, you have to find ways in which you obtain their labor without depleting your small capital of $100.

How do you go about this? Offer non-cash rewards. This could be in the form of:

> Joint ventures. You can choose to form a joint venture with someone who has the skill or can provide the labor you are looking for. A joint venture is simply a project-based partnership. You can then share profits from the project based on the agreed-upon formula. This way, you won't have to spend your cash on wages.

> Shareholding. You can create shares of your enterprise. Then, issue shares equivalent to the value of wages sacrificed by those who are working for you.

➢ Tokens. Tokens are like shares. However, they are not a form of ownership and are saleable. A typical example is the cryptocurrency token.

➢ Prizes. For certain jobs, you can convert their performance into a contest where the winner gets a certain prize. This can be among friends. The prize can be non-monetary, such as a special hand-made gift or even a certificate.

➢ Debt. This should be the last resort if other non-cash rewards are not appealing to those you want to work for you. A debt simply postpones the cash reward instead of substituting it.

#8 Take advantage of free or cheap offers

Many free offers exist that can make starting your business quite easy. For example, when it comes to e-commerce, there are many free e-commerce platforms (such as WooCommerce and Magento), free hosting offers (such as wordpress.com and blogger.com), and free social media platforms for building your network and community (such as Facebook, Twitter, LinkedIn, Pinterest, Instagram, and Snapchat). Take advantage of cheap offers such as discounts, rebates, and others.

#9 Opt for a longer credit repayment period

As a teen, you may get some soft loans from your parents, relatives, or friends. In case you decide to leverage your business, opt for credit with a longer repayment period so that your cashflow is not constrained. You need working capital.

The more cash you have on your hands, the greater the potential for a multiplier effect. Maximize cash inflows while restricting cash outflows.

#10 Give preference to a business that is easy to scale up at a minimal fixed cost

What you need most is to avoid stagnation. Your need your $100 investment to grow exponentially so that, eventually, you not only become self-employed but also an entrepreneur.

Some businesses cannot grow without consuming lots of fixed costs such as rent, labor, etc. On the other hand, other businesses, such as selling digital products (e.g. apps and e-books) can easily scale up without costing you additional fixed costs. Other factors being the same, give preference to those businesses whose fixed costs won't expand as much as the business scales up.

Chapter 16: Tips on How to Penetrate the Global Marketplace

Scaling up your small business is important if you want to focus on entrepreneurship. Luckily, with the advent of the internet, scaling up has become much easier than in the olden days. With the internet, the world is at your fingertips. Some of the leading global marketplaces where you can pitch your products and services include:

➢ Amazon

➢ eBay

➢ Airbnb

➢ Etsy

Tips for the Amazon Marketplace

The best way to leverage Amazon for your business is by fulfillment. Fulfillment by Amazon (FBA) simply means letting Amazon fulfill an order from your customer on your behalf. In essence, it is outsourcing your fulfillment service/function to Amazon. Amazon FBA is essentially an end-to-end fulfillment service that takes care of:

➢ Warehousing

➢ Order processing

➢ Billing

➢ Returns and exchanges

➢ Payment processing

➢ Customer service support

How does Amazon FBA work?

Fulfillment by Amazon works through the following steps:

Step 1: Deliver your product to Amazon (via your Private Label supplier).

Step 2: Amazon stores your products in its inventory (thus undertaking basic inventory management).

Step 3: Customers buy your product (via the Amazon product page).

Step 4: Amazon selects and packs the product on your behalf.

Step 5: Amazon delivers the product to your customer (including shipping).

Step 6: Amazon bills the customer and receives payment on your behalf.

Step 7: Amazon channels payment to your bank account.

Tips for the Airbnb Marketplace

Airbnb is a famous online marketplace that offers collaborative consumption and the sharing of hospitality services by enabling guests and travelers to rent or lease short-term lodging facilities. This includes apartment rentals, homestays, vacation rentals, hotel rooms, or hostel beds, among so many others.

Why choose Airbnb?

Airbnb is one of the biggest online marketplaces of its kind. It has over 3 million lodging listings in over 190 countries around the globe. It is trusted by both hosts and guests.

How does it work?

Both hosts and guests meet online on the airbnb.com marketplace. The host creates a profile (commonly known as a listing). The listing comprises the description of the lodging property including its photo, its key features, location, surrounding amenities and infrastructure, landmarks, what is on offer, etc.

The guest checks out the market, searching for rentals based on location and size description (apartment, private room, shared room, etc). Once the guest settles on a certain listing, they prompt an offer to the host via the platform's communication system. If the host accepts, the booking is done.

After the booking is done, both the host and the guest arrange to meet to facilitate occupancy of the place by the guest and to ensure that the guest's needs are well attended to.

At the end, both the host and guest can make independent reviews about their experience on the platform. This greatly helps to boost quality, reputation, and trust.

How to become a host

Airbnb is a great platform for hosts. The following are the main steps you need to take to become a host:

- ➤ Decide on the property you want to rent
- ➤ Prepare it for hosting
- ➤ Sign up for hosting with Airbnb.com
- ➤ Prepare your listing
- ➤ Receive bookings
- ➤ Welcome guests
- ➤ Get paid

Tips for the Etsy Marketplace

Etsy is the world's biggest online community marketplace for craftwork. It is a global community where creative minds express and exchange value for their intrinsically creative solutions using marketing tools.

The nature of Etsy

Etsy is:

- ➤ A community of creative people interacting and expressing their creativity
- ➤ A marketplace where creative people gather to exchange value in creative solutions
- ➤ An e-commerce platform with tools that facilitate the exchange of creative ideas

Types of creative solutions

There are two main types of creative solutions available on Etsy:

- ➤ Handmade crafts
- ➤ Vintage crafts

Handmade crafts

These are non-manufactured crafts. They are made through the work of one's creative hands as an expression of one's creative ideas.

Vintage crafts

Etsy considers a product as vintage only if it is at least 20 years old.

How to open an Etsy storefront

Opening an Etsy storefront is easy. The following are the main steps to opening your Etsy storefront:

1. Gather sufficient information about Etsy

2. Open an account

3. Open your shop

4. Start marketing

5. Run your shop

6. Create and expand your community

Tips for App Marketplaces

Great apps are in high demand. You can create mobile apps, web apps, or desktop apps. You can also create hybrid apps for both mobile and web or different OS (Operating Systems such as Android, iOS, Windows, Linux, etc.).

If you are not an app developer and are not interested in becoming one, you can choose to be an app seller. Simply buy apps and sell them like any other product.

Tips for creating great apps

1. Have a great picture in mind.

91

2. Focus on your target niche.

3. Create an effective design and implementation strategy.

4. Keep It Sleek and Simple.

➤ Create a strong first impression, especially for mobile apps. Users decide in a split-second whether to try out your app or not.

➤ Design a clutter-free user interface. Less is more. When it comes to mobile, portability matters. A heavily cluttered user interface weighs down the users.

➤ Make it accessible and more comfortable. Let the hyperlinks be easily accessible. Make the buttons large enough to easily click or tap. Make the click or touch feather-soft.

5. Leverage the advantages of the latest technology. Using the latest technology means that your app has the potential fora longer lifespan. It also means that your app is going to ride the new wave.

6. Seamless integration across devices. Users should be able to get the same feel irrespective of the screen size, type of device, or OS.

7. Keep It Lightning Light. When it comes to mobile apps, speed is of critical importance. Users don't want to waste their time on slow and sluggish loading speed. They want apps that are superfast. This is what boosts user experience.

8. Stress-test your app. Many apps simply collapse due to minor stresses such as low bandwidth, light shocks (such as the gadget falling), persistent clicks, frequent OS updates, etc. Test your app under different strenuous conditions to establish its tolerance limits. Seek to boost the app's tolerance level.

9. Make it a solution. The app should be able to solve user problems. It should be designed as a solution. Thus, you have to identify user problems, challenges, and pain-points and create an app that solves them.

10. Let it create an emotional connection. The app should have an emotional feel. The choice of colors, fonts, navigations, displays, etc. should create an emotional connection to the app. Emotional connections boost user satisfaction, build loyalty, and increase sales.

Tips for marketing your apps

If you are an app developer, that's great. But if you are not, that shouldn't stop you from selling apps. You can buy them and sell them. Alternatively, if you have some money, you can hire a developer for you. So not being a developer should not stop you from trading in apps.

The following tips will help you greatly market your apps:

- Talk and talk about it. Tell everyone who cares to read and listen to you about your app. Write about it on your blog. Demonstrate it on your vlog. Share it with people on your social media.
- Do email marketing. Send emails to potential leads.
- Do affiliate marketing. Employ people to market on your behalf while earning commissions. Use affiliate marketing platforms such as Clickbank, Rakuten, Commission Junction, and others.
- Build a community on social media. Use social media to build a community. Twitter is ideal for news updates such as improved features, new features, new versions, new staff members, new collaboration, etc. Facebook is ideal for interactions and lead nurturing. Whatsapp is ideal for closing sales. YouTube is ideal for product demos.
- Take the freemium approach. Offer a free version and a paid version. Offer a limited free trial full version. This is an opportunity for "doubting Thomases" to try it out before making a decision. And they are the majority, so prove it to them.
- Use both one-time-purchases and subscriptions. One-time-purchases are often more expensive for many potential customers, yet it's the most ideal for premium customers. To improve on affordability while expanding the market, offer subscription-based sales. Subscriptions

are affordable, but let them make economic sense, at least in terms of frequency and associated costs of acquisition, installation, billing, and payment processing. You can let users subscribe monthly, quarterly, semi-annually, annually, or even biennially. The shorter the period, the more expensive the subscription should be.

➤ Offer freebies. We humans, by nature, love free things. They attract us. They are magnetic. We easily fall into the trap of freebies. Leverage this innate human psychology to boost your sales. Freebies can be in the form of free samples, promo code, rebates, cashbacks, discounts, etc.

Best marketplaces for buying and selling apps

Once you have developed an app (be it a desktop app, web app, or mobile app), the next challenge is where to sell it. Luckily, there are well-established marketplaces for you to sell your apps, especially web and mobile ones. The following are some of the leading app marketplaces:

Envato

Envato ranks as the top marketplace for all kinds of small apps. Most apps range between $5 and $100. Thus, if you intend to sell an app, create or buy one that can be priced within that range.

Envato has several specialized markets in addition to other functions. For example, apart from buying and selling apps (via CodeCanyon), there are also tutorials (Envato Tuteplus) on Envato. There are also design platforms (Envato Studio).

CodeCanyon

CodeCanyon is an apps market under the Envato umbrella. It a place to buy and sell all kinds of apps. Apps are typically priced within the range of $5 to $100. Some can be lower and others can be much higher.

Types of Apps Sold:

➢ Desktop: Java, C++, Ruby, Python, VB.NET

➢ Mobile: Android, iOS, Hybrid

➢ Web: PHP, Java, C#, Javascript, Ruby

➢ Plugins for: WordPress, Drupal, Joomla, Magenta, Prestashop, osCommerce, OpenCart, WooCommerce, WP-eCommerce, Google Chrome, Firefox

➢ Others: Script files, templates, themes, etc.

Codester

Codester is a marketplace where both mobile and web apps are sold.

Types of Apps Sold:

➢ Desktop: Java, C++, Ruby, Python, VB.NET

➢ Mobile: Android, iOS, Hybrid

➢ Web: PHP, Java, C#, Javascript, Ruby

- ➤ Plugins for: WordPress, Drupal, Joomla, Magenta, Prestashop, osCommerce, OpenCart, WooCommerce, WP-eCommerce
- ➤ Plugins for: WordPress, Drupal, Joomla, Magenta, Prestashop, osCommerce, OpenCart, WooCommerce, WP-eCommerce, Google Chrome, Firefox
- ➤ Others: Script files, templates, themes, etc.

Other app marketplaces:

- ➤ SellMyApp
- ➤ Sellify
- ➤ FetchApp
- ➤ Gumroad
- ➤ EasyDigitalDownloads
- ➤ SendOwl
- ➤ PayLoads
- ➤ PayToolbox
- ➤ SellWire
- ➤ CreativeMarket
- ➤ Selz
- ➤ eJunkie

App developer tutorials

If you want to be an app developer, there are plenty of sites that offer tutorials. Some offer free tutorials while others offer paid tutorials. Paid tutorials are often more elaborate and in-depth.

However, as a beginner, free tutorials can ground you well. All you need to know is which are the good sites to learn from, as there are many crappy sites out there on the internet. Here is a list of a few of them to get started.

Free app developer tutorials
In case you would like to learn how to develop apps, the following are the great sites where you can learn for free.

W3Schools

Courses offered:

➢ Web scripts: HTML, CSS, Javascript, PHP, ASP, Node.js

➢ Mobile: jQuery

➢ General programming: Java, Python, C++, C#, SQL, Raspberry PI

TutorialsPoint

Courses offered:

➢ Web scripts: HTML, CSS, Javascript, PHP

➢ Mobile: jQuery, Android, Swift, React Native, Xamarin, Native Script, Flutter, Ionic, etc.

➢ General programming; Java, Python, Dart, Go, C++, C#, SQL, Electron, VBScript, etc.

➢ Latest technologies: Machine Learning, Artificial Intelligence, Blockchain

Guru99

Courses offered:

- ➢ Web scripts: HTML, CSS, Javascript, PHP, Angularjs
- ➢ Mobile: jQuery, Kotlin
- ➢ General programming: Java, Python, Dart, Go, C++, C#, SQL, Kotlin

Paid app developer tutorials

Udemy

Udemy is a popular tutorial marketplace that has diverse courses. It is one of the cheapest tutorial sites. Other than coding/app development, Udemy offers many other courses for a price.

Let's look at courses offered that are relevant to the app development niche.

Courses offered:

- ➢ Web scripts: HTML, CSS, Javascript, PHP
- ➢ Mobile: jQuery, Android, Swift, React Native, Xamarin, Native Script, Flutter, Ionic, etc.
- ➢ General programming: Java, Python, Dart, Go, C++, C#,SQL, Electron, VBScript, etc.
- ➢ Latest technologies: Machine Learning, Artificial Intelligence, Blockchain

LinkedIn Learning (Lynda)

LinkedIn Learning, formerly Lynda, is a high-quality learning marketplace where you can learn a lot of subjects beyond just coding. It is distinguished for the quality of its lessons.

The following are some of the courses offered within the app development niche.

Courses offered:

➢ Web scripts: HTML, CSS, Javascript, PHP

➢ Mobile: jQuery, Android, Swift, React Native, Xamarin, Native Script, Flutter, Ionic, etc.

➢ General programming: Java, Python, Dart, Go, C++, C#, SQL, Electron, VBScript, etc.

➢ Latest technologies: Machine Learning, Artificial Intelligence, Blockchain

Skillshare

Skillshare is a general site that offers more lessons than coding. As the name suggests, this is a social learning platform where people join to share skills. For example, I teach you coding, you teach me Chinese. However, not everyone has sharable skills and so those who have no skill to share can pay to learn. The only disadvantage of skillshare is the quality of the trainers. You are not certain of the quality of the person training you. You could get a great trainer and you could also get an inexperienced trainer. So it's up to you to do the vetting.

Coding Platforms

Coding platforms are ones that provide you with a space to write your code. They are popularly known as Integrated Development Environments (IDE). There are many IDEs out there, some online and others offline; some general and some specialized.

The following is a list of some of the popular ones:

Online IDEs

In case you have stable high-speed internet and you like moving around, then using an online IDE can be a great solution. This means that you will be able to access your coding project wherever you are and can pick up from where you left off.

Common online IDEs are:

➢ jDoodle

➢ Monaco

➢ Codeshare

Offline IDEs

General programming:

➢ Visual Studio

➢ Eclipse

➢ Aptana Studio

- ➤ NetBeans
- ➤ IntelliJ (not free)
- ➤ Dreamweaver (not free)

I recommend Visual Studio, as it is not only free but also modern with plenty of plugins for many programming languages.

Mobile Programming:
- ➤ Android Studio (for developing Android apps)
- ➤ XCode (for developing iOS apps)
- ➤ Atom
- ➤ Apache Cordova
- ➤ Webstorm (not free)
- ➤ Ionic Studio (for developing Ionic apps, hybrid apps)

If you want to be an Android developer, then Android Studio is right for you. If you plan to be an OS developer, then XCode is right for you. If you want to develop hybrid apps (that run on both Android and iOS), then Ionic Studio is right for you. Alternatively, you can jump into Flutter—the new hybrid language that you can build using either Android Studio (recommended) or Visual Studio.

Web programming:
- ➤ Atom
- ➤ Brackets

➤ <u>Komodo</u>

➤ <u>Webstorm (not free)</u>

Tips on Tutorial Marketplaces

You can make money selling tutorials, be it tutorial products or tutorial services.

The following are some common tutorial products that you can sell.

DIY tutorials

The following are common media that you can use to sell your DIY tutorial products:

➤ Videos

➤ Podcasts

➤ Webinars

➤ Notes

How-to tutorials

The following are common media that you can use to sell your "how-to» tutorial products:

➤ Videos

➤ Podcasts

➤ Webinars

➤ Notes

If you have tutorials that you want to sell, there are several tutorial marketplaces where you can sell your tutorials. The following are some of the top tutoring sites that do not require you to have a college degree or advanced degree.

Udemy

Udemy is one of the oldest online educational platforms. It has been around for several years. It has a huge array of multi-disciplinary courses. You are more likely to find all the skills you are looking for on Udemy.

Key platform features

➢ User-friendly search facility

➢ Individual and business options

➢ Prominent "become an instructor" button

➢ Top courses are given prominence on the front page

Reputation

Udemy is highly respected. It is positively regarded by millions of learners who have gone through it and the hundreds of trainers who have entrusted it as a means of delivering their lessons.

Mode of study

There are many different trainers on Udemy. Each trainer is specialized in a particular skill set.

You choose your trainer by going through the trainer's profile whereby you have access to the trainer's learning materials.

Skills offered

➢ Web Design

➢ Mobile Development

➢ Animation/GIFs

➢ Music Production

➢ Social Media

➢ Calligraphy

➢ Photoshop

➢ Photography

➢ Cinematography

➢ Productivity

➢ Illustration

➢ Instagram

➢ Cost

➢ Free to register

➢ Price depends on your chosen course

➢ Plenty of free courses

Earning opportunity

Earn as a trainer: Most of the trainers on Udemy are independent contractors and work on a freelance basis. They are not employed by Udemy or anyone. They too love freedom, flexibility, and unlimited opportunities for growth.

You too can become a trainer by offering your current skills. I started earning on Udemy by offering my Spanish language skills. I am bilingual—English and Spanish. Check the skills you already have and repackage them for sale. They could include specialized cooking (culinary art), drawing, etc.

The best way to start is to enroll for training (most likely about what you already know) to see how your trainers deliver so that you can emulate them and, if possible, do better than them.

Earn as an affiliate: Udemy also provides opportunities for market-savvy students and anyone else to earn by simply referring others to the platform.

Pros
 ➢ Up-to-date, on-demand skills
 ➢ Opportunity to earn as an instructor
 ➢ Opportunity to share skills
 ➢ Lots of free courses
 ➢ 10-day free trial

Cons
 ➢ Courses are relatively short
 ➢ Language support is limited
 ➢ Limited video captioning
 ➢ Little help in finding the best trainer

Bottom line
Udemy has an expansive catalog of courses. You can hardly miss getting the skills you are looking for. It is a great

platform for entrepreneurial learners who want to learn and also earn at the same time on the same platform.

Instructables
Instructables is a large site with plenty of DIY (Do-It-Yourself) craft projects.

Key platform features
➢ Focus on DIY craft projects

➢ Great forum

➢ Easy search facility

➢ Great project samples

Reputation
Instructables has been in existence for a long time. It is highly reputable as a source of instruction for a wide variety of DIY projects.

Skills offered
➢ Photography

➢ Design

➢ Jewelry

➢ 3D printing

➢ Electronics

➢ Robotics

➢ Embroidery

➢ Knitting

➢ Woodwork

- ➢ Animation/GIFs
- ➢ Calligraphy
- ➢ Photoshop
- ➢ Cinematography
- ➢ Illustration
- ➢ Software
- ➢ Cooking
- ➢ Crafts

Cost

Instructables is free to register.

Earning opportunity

The only direct earning opportunity on Instructables is through contests from which you earn prize amounts and gifts.

However, there are many indirect earning opportunities. You can learn how to make unique things on Instructables. Once you make them, you can sell them on eBay or Etsy. You can also create Instructables lessons on YouTube, which you can monetize to earn through advertisements posted on your video. Also, you can create a free blog either on Blogger or WordPress where you can post your lessons to monetize them through Adsense advertisements. Furthermore, your lessons are a great way to market yourself to potential clients who might hire you to make them some unique crafts.

Pros

Instructables is one place where you can find crazy DIY projects. As a beginner, you can easily get started as the platform is simple to join and use. Furthermore, the lessons range from as low as K-12 level, right through to university level. There is something for everybody.

Cons

Though there are great opportunities for utilizing your skills acquired from the platform to earn elsewhere, there are few earning opportunities on the platform itself.

Bottom line

Instructables is a great place to learn practical skills if you are a hands-on person who loves DIY projects. There is great potential to start as an online entrepreneur selling your crafts through your blog, eBay, and Etsy, among other craft selling platforms.

Skillshare

Skillshare, as the name suggests, is focused on providing skill-focused training to its students. The core concept is the sharing of skills amongst platform users.

Key platform features

➤ Unlimited access to courses

➤ Subscription-based

➤ Strong community

➤ Courses are rated based on student recommendations

Reputation
Skillshare is a reputable online educational platform that is best known for the "freelance" approach to teaching and learning. You get to choose a specific skill that you want to learn and find an instructor who will specifically deliver that.

Skills offered
There are plenty of courses for skills in high demand. The following are some of the skills offered:

➤ Design
➤ Business
➤ Technology
➤ Photography
➤ Film
➤ Writing
➤ Crafts
➤ Culinary Arts
➤ Web Design
➤ Mobile Development
➤ Animation/GIFs
➤ Calligraphy
➤ Photoshop
➤ Photography
➤ Cinematography

- ➢ Illustration
- ➢ Software

Cost

Skillshare has two pricing options:

- ➢ Free
- ➢ Premium - $9

The free option has advertisements included. The premium option has no advertisements. That's the only distinction.

Earning opportunity

Earn as a trainer: Skillshare offers a great earning opportunity for anyone who has a skill to share. You can create a course for what you already know and offer it for sale. Even if you don't have advanced knowledge of your skill, provided that you have mastered the basics, you can make a course out of that. Many beginners are just looking for those basics.

Earn as an affiliate: You can earn $10 for every new user you successfully refer to the platform.

Pros

- ➢ Unlimited access to thousands of courses
- ➢ Plenty of courses to learn from
- ➢ Up-to-date skills on the market

- ➢ Extremely affordable
- ➢ A simple platform for easy navigation
- ➢ Earning opportunity for learners

Cons

Instructors are not vetted, so some of the courses may not be up to standards.

Bottom line

Skillshare is a great place to start if you want to learn a new skill. It is also a place where you can learn different skills of interest at one flat rate. For those who want to earn, Skillshare is a great place to market your skill as a course. It provides both learning and earning opportunities.

Universal Class

Universal Class is a unique learning platform that blends school-based courses with modern non-school-based courses.

Key platform features

- ➢ Conspicuous course catalog
- ➢ A dropdown list of areas of study
- ➢ Subscription-based
- ➢ Featured courses displayed on the front page

Reputation

Universal Class has a good reputation in its field as an online educational platform and has a huge selection of courses and skills on offer. It is registered with the Better Business Bureau (BBB). It is also accredited by the International Association of Continuing Education and Training (IACET).

Skills offered

There are so many skills offered. The following are just a few:

➤ Finance, accounting and bookkeeping

➤ Computer training

➤ Crafts and hobbies

➤ Web development

➤ Writing skills

➤ Entrepreneurship

Cost

There are four cost options:

➤ Platinum monthly - $59 for the first month and then $29 for subsequent months

➤ Platinum 1 Year - $189 for one year

➤ Platinum 2 Years - $299 for two years

➤ Platinum 3 Years - $399 for three years

Earning opportunity

The great thing with Universal Class is that there are a variety of courses. You can even package your great hobby into a course and offer to teach it. The downside is that, unlike other platforms, you have to submit an application that is subject to the administration's approval or disapproval. You are simply not guaranteed.

Pros
➤ There are plenty of offerings, both traditional and market-driven on-demand courses.
➤ You learn at your own pace.
➤ You can take single independent courses or a Continuing Education Unit (CEU).

Cons
➤ No voice interaction with the instructor, as the mode of communication is the message board and email
➤ Extremely limited earning opportunities for learners

Bottom line
Universal Class is a great place to learn a new market-driven, on-demand skill. It provides an opportunity for one to become an instructor, as long as one is skilled enough in what they want to offer.

Website: universalclass.com

Other great tutorials sites:
➤ VIPKid
➤ Brainfuse
➤ Chegg Tutors
➤ QKids
➤ MagicEars

Tips for Online Freelance Marketplaces

The world of independent work is expanding day by day. Millions of people are working as online freelancers, an occupation preferred by many because of the freedom and flexibility it grants.

With freelancing, you can choose to work part-time or on a contract-by-contract basis. This way, you can still afford to study and even work on the side project that you want to grow.

Freelancing skills

Some of the most sought online freelancing skills are:

➢ Writing

➢ Translation

➢ Graphic design

➢ Coding/programming

➢ Virtual assistance

➢ Voice-overs

Freelancing marketplaces

There are many freelancing marketplaces where you can earn money from selling your skill. These freelancing marketplaces can be classified into the following broad categories:

➢ General freelancing marketplaces

➤ Specialized freelancing marketplaces

General freelancing marketplaces
There are freelance marketplaces that are not niche-specific.
They appeal across many fields. The following are the most
popular general freelancing marketplaces where you can sell
your skills or even find skills to collaborate with or employ
for your business:

➤ Upwork

➤ Freelancer

➤ Fiverr

➤ Guru

➤ PeoplePerHour

➤ Workana

Specialized freelancing marketplaces
Specialized marketplaces are ones focused on a set of skills
within a specific niche such as design, coding, acting, music,
etc.

Design skills marketplaces
These are marketplaces that focus on design and where those
who want to employ or sell their design skills meet. The
following are the most popular design skills marketplaces:

➤ 99Designs

➤ EnvatoStudio

- ➤ DesignCrowd
- ➤ DesignContest
- ➤ Expert360

Coding skills marketplaces

These are marketplaces that cater to skills requirements for the coding/programming niche. Here is where you can sell or hire coding skills:

- ➤ Toptal
- ➤ TopCoder
- ➤ Expert360
- ➤ GitHub Jobs
- ➤ Stack Overflow
- ➤ Gun.io

Affiliate Marketplaces

Affiliate marketing is a marketing arrangement characterized by one entity carrying out marketing activities on behalf of another entity through a neutral intermediary.

This means there are three parties involved in the marketing effort. The promoter (publisher/affiliate), the seller (product creator/merchant), and the neutral intermediary (a platform/affiliate network).

Parties of affiliate marketing

Affiliate marketing transactions involve the following key parties:

1. **Product Merchant**: Also known as the product creator/product owner, a product merchant is the owner of the product that needs to be promoted.

2. **Affiliate Network Platform**: This is a platform that provides tools, links, and analytics for products being promoted. The affiliate network acts as a link between the product merchant and the affiliate marketer.

3. **Affiliate Merchant**: This is a business entity that dedicates itself to promoting products, traffic, and brand awareness through a network of affiliate sites. As such, they create various kinds of ads including text links ads, static banner ads, flash banners ads, video ads, and sometimes a combination to be placed on affiliate websites. To achieve this, an affiliate merchant uses an affiliate network platform.

4. **Affiliate Marketer (Affiliate/Publisher)**: This is the owner of an affiliate website on which an affiliate merchant's ads and links are placed. The affiliate marketer endeavors to promote the product to the target audience through content (such as articles, product reviews, how-to instructions, product comparisons, etc.).

5. **Consumer (Customer/Buyer)**: This is the person who accesses the product being promoted by an affiliate via affiliate links and successfully buys the product.

Most of the time, affiliate merchants have their in-house platform. However, in some cases, affiliate merchants hire an external affiliate network platform. It is not uncommon for the affiliate network platform and affiliate merchant to be treated the same. But technically, they are not the same.

In this book, we use the terms "affiliate network platform" and "affiliate merchant" interchangeably. In some instances, we will use "affiliate network provider" to refer to a combination of both. Nonetheless, it must be noted that an affiliate merchant can't work without an affiliate network platform. Thus, whenever "affiliate merchant" is mentioned, "affiliate network platform" is implied and vice versa.

How affiliate marketing works

The following steps provide a glimpse into how affiliate marketing works:

1. A merchant approaches an affiliate network provider to be helped to promote their product.

2. Both the affiliate merchant and the network provider agree on their respective earnings. They also agree on what to pay affiliates.

3. The network provider creates a product-specific link generation system that automatically generates links based on the product merchant's details (product name details) and affiliate marketer's details (Affiliate ID).

4. The affiliate marketer approaches the network provider, gets registered, and is provided with auto-generated links based on their registration details to place on their site/blog.

5. The affiliate marketer hyperlinks certain parts of the content/space using provided links.

6. The affiliate publishes their content on the blog, which attracts the attention of readers.

7. The reader goes through the content and, if convinced of the need to buy the product being promoted, decides to click on the affiliate hyperlink.

8. Once the reader (potential buyer) clicks on the hyperlink, they are redirected to the product's page at the product merchant's site.

9. If the customer decides to buy the product, this becomes a successful sale through the affiliate's marketing effort. The details of the purchase are recorded both by the affiliate network and the product merchant.

10. On a successful sale, the affiliate's account is credited with the amount due. How soon that is done depends on the security period. Most affiliate networks provide a security period of fewer than 30 days. The security period ensures that the affiliate is not paid if the customer returns the product later on to claim a refund. The security period depends on the product merchant's return policy, plus the waiting period added on by the affiliate network.

Affiliate marketing platforms

Over time, certain marketing platforms have won resilience and progress to become the platforms of choice for most product merchants and affiliate marketers.

The following are the top five affiliate marketing platforms that you can choose from as a starting point as you continue to evaluate each based on the kind of niche you are focused on:

➢ Commission Junction
➢ Clickbank
➢ ShareAsale
➢ Linkshare
➢ Amazon Associates

Unlike others, Amazon Associates focuses only on products sold on the Amazon marketplace. Thus, it is more of a merchant-driven affiliate platform. It is the most preferred affiliate platform if you are marketing products on Amazon already. However, if you are not marketing products already on the Amazon platform, then you will have to consider the first four platforms.

Criteria for choosing your niche product

Finding products to market is an important endeavor that will determine how far you succeed in your affiliate marketing goals. The following criteria will help you decide on the most appropriate products:

1. **Choose a product niche that aligns with your passion**: Blogging is about passion. Thus, you have to choose a product niche that aligns with your passion so that you can match it with your content. As an affiliate marketer, you are a publisher. Trying to publish content that doesn't align with your passion will cause you to burn out sooner than later. Passion is what drives you and will help you continue writing against all odds. Affiliate marketing is not a sprint race, but a marathon.

The focus is on long-term gains rather than short-term gains. Many give up and quit too soon because they were disappointed that the product that they were trying to market didn't pick up as soon as they expected. This won't be the case if you are blogging from your passion, as your income is simply a fringe benefit.

2. **Choose a product niche that is available on your preferred network platform**: Not all network platforms are the same. Some are reputable and match your needs and some do not. Once you have decided on your best platform, check the range of products offered and if your product niche fits. If it does, that's great; if not, find the next best alternative to your preferred platform or product niche.

3. **Choose a profitable product**: Profitability of a product is determined by the commission offered (both in terms of rate and amount), how fast the product is likely to turnover (the frequency of sales per given period, e.g. per month), and your minimum expected rate of return (return on your investment, e.g. hosting and publishing costs). Different product merchants have different rates of commission. Yet different network platforms offer different rates of commission on the same product. So when you decide on the most profitable

product, research to find the best commission rates among the best platforms.

4. **Choose a product that you can continue marketing in the long-term**: Seasonal and one-off products are not ideal for your affiliate marketing if you are just beginning to establish yourself, as they dry out soon. If you want your affiliate marketing endeavor to be an investment, choose products that are going to continue having consistent demand for several years to come. This way, you can publish evergreen content; that is, content that remains relevant for many years to come. You will continue earning from the continued promotion of your affiliate links due to this content for as long as the product remains on the market and the affiliate link remains valid.

Chapter 17: Tips on Creating a Multiplier Effect

You want your $100 investment to grow exponentially. The worst thing is stagnation. You are too young to remain stunted. You are here to learn and grow, your age is all about growth. And so should your $100 investment.

How do you exponentially multiply the growth of your $100 into potential millions?

This is the one-million-dollar question. The answer rests in five surprisingly simple tips!

The Top Five Multiplier Tips

The following are the top five tips that you can employ to maximize the multiplier effect of your $100 worth.

Tip #1 Invest in skills

As a teenager, skill is the most important capital that you have. Money is just the key to unlocking your skill potential. Seek new skills and advance the skills that you already have. Skill development has the greatest multiplier effect. The more productive skills you acquire, the greater the potential to multiply gains from your $100 investment. The biggest benefit of investing in skills is that *a skill is a lifetime multiplier*.

Tip #2 Invest in gathering productive information

We are in the information age. Information can make the difference between your business growing or remaining stunted, even collapsing. Information can help you acquire cheaper sources of input and can help you obtain premium customers, expanding your profit margin.

The good thing is that with the internet, all you need is to spend more time carrying out in-depth research on your suppliers and markets.

Tip #3 Invest in building a strong business and social network

People=money. This is the most obvious secret. Money doesn't grow on trees, it comes from people's pockets. This means the more people you have access to, the greater the potential to make money.

Yet, like everything else, quality matters. Establish a productive business and social network. Social capital is important to your business. It is from the community that you can obtain customers. Everyone is a potential customer, what makes someone not your customer is either your lack of knowledge of the person or simply your lack of a need-satisfying product or service on your end.

Tip #4 Invest in time management

Time is money. Don't mismanage it. When you are a teenager, you don't have loads of cash on you, but you do have loads of time. Take advantage of it. Make your time more productive and utilize it to advance your business.

Tip #5 Invest in partnerships and joint ventures, as opposed to sole proprietorship

If it takes you $100 as a sole proprietor to start a business venture, it will take $50 each for two of you in a partnership. And it will take only $25 if you are four partners. Partnership frees up more cash towards operational costs, which is directly responsible for generating revenue. You are more likely to breakeven and soar exponentially if you have more free working capital, than when most of your funds are absorbed by starting capital.

Chapter 18: Tips on How to Cheaply Start Your E-commerce Website

The biggest advantage of e-commerce is the low cost of capital. The second biggest advantage is the wider market access. The third biggest advantage is the ease by which you can quickly scale up.

There are many more advantages that can be best discussed in a separate book on e-commerce, but the advantages mentioned here are powerful enough to persuade you to have an e-commerce presence.

Being on a shoestring budget of $100 or less, cost becomes an extremely sensitive factor, so you need to find ways to start your e-commerce venture without burning a significant proportion of your $100 budget. The following tips will help you achieve your objectives.

Tip #1 Find a cheap domain registrar and TLD (less than $3)

Certain domains sell cheaply. Popular TLDs such as .com, .net, .co are not cheap but some domain registrars can sell them at less than $3 as a special offer for the first year. If you get one of those three TLDs at less than $3, then that is a great bargain to start with.

If you can't find popular TLDs at $3 or less, you can opt for new TLDs that go for as cheap as $0.99. But you have to be careful about the reputation of the registrar so that you don't opt for a seemingly cheap TLD that locks you in for years. Namecheap is the best and most reliable domain registrar.

Tip #2 Find a cheap website host (typically less than $5 per month)

When it comes to web hosting, the price is not the main guide. Quality counts more. You have to strike a balance between quality and price. Some hosts are very cheap, but you will regret it when customers are turned away at the shopping cart step due to slow speed.

Bluehost, A2Hosting, Scalahosting, and Hostgator are some of the best webhosting companies out there. Almost all of them offer a starting package of less than $5 for the first month, but thereafter, some go for as high as $15 a month. Don't be deceived by the first-month offer. Scalahosting looks cheapest for standard rate (without first-month discount) at $5.95.

In case you decide to use WooCommerce as your e-commerce engine, it will be cheaper to go with WordPress hosting. Namecheap offers you WordPress hosting at a flat rate of

$3.88 per month with a first-month discounted rate of just $0.01 (as of04/17/2020).

Tip #3 Install a free e-commerce platform (WooCommerce preferred)

There are several e-commerce platforms to choose from. These include Magenta, Prestashop, WooCommerce, OpenCart, OSCommerce, WP-eCommerce, among others.

However, as a starter, it is preferable to use WooCommerce as it is integrated with WordPress. It is also easy to install. Furthermore, WordPress hosting being cheap (especially at Namecheap), it will cost you less overall.

The other advantage of WooCommerce is that as it's integrated with WordPress, you can easily blog and trade on the same platform. This is important for SEO marketing, as your blog can market your e-commerce site.

Tip #4 Rather than hiring a web developer, save money by investing your time in learning how to tweak your e-commerce site

Hiring a web developer could cost you a lot. Yet within just a few hours, you can install and tweak your WordPress site.

You can learn on the job and seek help from places such as Stack Overflow. You can also Google for solutions, provided you properly frame your question.

Tip #5 To avoid stock costs, start with dropshipping and arbitrage

Dropshipping and arbitrage don't require you to hold stock. Stocking is expensive. If you want to buy and sell goods, avoid stocking, as it could inconveniently restrict your small capital.

Tip #6 For intangible items, start with selling e-books and apps

If you plan to start selling digital items, e-books are the easiest to start with. You can write them to sell. If you cannot write, hire someone to write for you. Start with short e-books of 3500-5000 words, as they will cost you less in terms of writing or hiring a ghostwriter. You could spend about $40 towards hiring a ghostwriter for a short e-book. However, make sure that you have a high-selling topic, so do adequate research.

To even save more on your capital expenditure, you can opt to sell e-books and apps on a commission basis as an affiliate marketer. You will just spend a little on creating your website. WordPress.com and Blogger.com are free blogs that you can use before deciding to host your own.

Tip #7 Market your e-commerce website on social media

Once you have your e-commerce website, market it on social media. Facebook, Twitter, and Instagram are great places to do so.

Tip #8 Cross-list your products on free marketplaces such as Amazon, eBay, Etsy, Facebook (shop), etc.

To optimize exposure, don't limit products to your e-commerce website. Cross list your products across other marketplaces such as Amazon, eBay, Etsy (for crafts), and even Facebook Shop.

You can also enroll a few of your products with affiliate marketing platforms such as ClickBank, Commission Junction, Amazon Affiliate, ShareAsale, and others.

You can also create special offers via coupons and cashbacks, and list them on Rakuten, SwagBucks, Cashbackbase, Amazon Coupons, etc. Make sure that you adjust your pricing accordingly.

Conclusion

Thank you for acquiring this book and reading it through to the end.

This book provides you with power—power to start and fuel your business. Information is power, and there is nothing more necessary.

With more than 100 business ideas that you can easily incubate into successful businesses, you are already spoilt for choices. Select one that blends your skills, passion, and creativity, plus the $100 at your disposal, and you'll have a business up and running in no time.

I hope you have been inspired by the information provided in this book to successfully start your business. I also hope that you have been inspired enough to recommend this guide to your friends so that they too can become teen entrepreneurs. Time is on your side—don't lose it to the vagaries of procrastination. Seize the moment and become a successful businessperson.

Again, thank you for reading this book. I wish you the best of luck in your business endeavors.

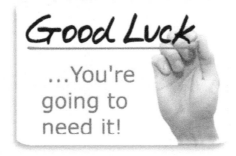

Made in the USA
Las Vegas, NV
11 January 2025

16223292R00080